KU-656-247

My Story Time
BIBLE

Retold by Sophie Piper *Illustrated by* Estelle Corke

LION
CHILDREN'S

To

LIBRARY SERVICES FOR SCHOOLS	
38003043092915	
Bertrams	11/05/2012
220.95	£8.99
LSS	

Text by Sophie Piper
Illustrations copyright © 2005 Estelle Corke
This edition copyright © 2012 Lion Hudson

The moral rights of the author and illustrator have been asserted

A Lion Children's Book
an imprint of
Lion Hudson plc
Wilkinson House, Jordan Hill Road,
Oxford OX2 8DR, England
www.lionhudson.com
ISBN 978 0 7459 6214 6

First edition 2012
1 3 5 7 9 10 8 6 4 2 0

All rights reserved

The Lord's Prayer as it appears in Common Worship: Services and Prayers for the
Church of England (Church House Publishing, 2000) is copyright © The English
Language Liturgical Consultation and is reproduced by permission of the publisher.

A catalogue record for this book is available from the British Library

Typeset in 20/25 Baskerville MT Schoolbook
Printed in China February 2012 (manufacturer LH17)

Distributed by:
UK: Marston Book Services Ltd, PO Box 269, Abingdon, Oxon OX14 4YN
USA: Trafalgar Square Publishing, 814 N Franklin Street, Chicago, IL 60610
USA Christian Market: Kregel Publications, PO Box 2607, Grand Rapids, MI 49

Contents

Stories from the Old Testament

Contents

Stories from the New Testament

God Makes
the World

Imagine a dark and stormy night.
Imagine a dark and stormy sea.
Before the world began, there was only darkness and storm.
Then God spoke: 'Let there be light.'
The light shone. God had made the very first day.

On the second day, God spoke
again: 'Let there be sky above and
sea below.' And there was.

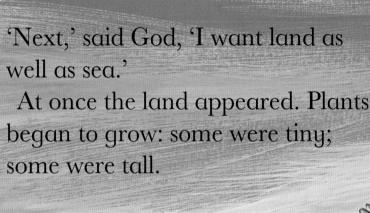

'Next,' said God, 'I want land as well as sea.'

At once the land appeared. Plants began to grow: some were tiny; some were tall.

'I have worked for three days, and everything is very good,' said God.

On day four, God made the sun.
'You must shine through the day,'
said God.

'Moon and the stars: I want you to shine at night.'

The whole universe did what God commanded.

Early on the fifth morning, God made all kinds of sea creatures: they came darting and diving through the waves.

Then God made the birds. They flapped and flew in the clear air.

On the sixth day, God made the animals – all kinds of amazing animals.

'And last,' said God, 'I shall make human beings. They will take care of my world.'

The six days of making were over.
It was time for a day of rest.

The first man was named Adam.
The first woman was named Eve.
God gave them a garden home.

'Everything is for you,' said God.
'There is just one tree you must not touch. If you eat its fruit, everything will go wrong.'

Adam and Eve were happy in their paradise home.

One day, a snake came and spoke to Eve. 'Did God say you mustn't eat the fruit here?' it asked.

'Only the fruit from one tree,' replied Eve. 'If we eat that, everything will go wrong.'

The snake twisted and wriggled. 'Not true!' it said. 'The fruit will make you as wise as God. Go on. Try it!'

Eve reached up. She picked the forbidden fruit. She ate some.

'It's good,' she said. 'I shall give some to Adam.'

Adam took a bite. Then he and Eve looked at each other.

'Oh dear,' they cried.

'We're both naked,' said Eve.

'And now, for the first time, that doesn't seem right,' said Adam.

They spent the day making clothes
from leaves. Then they heard God
coming. They hid among the trees.
  God called them.
  God found them.
  God saw what had happened, and
God was sad.

'Now everything must change,' said God. 'You must say goodbye to paradise. You must go out into the wide world. There you will work for all the things you need.'

God made Adam and Eve clothes to wear.

Sadly they walked out of the garden.

As they looked back, they saw an angel with a sword. The blade flashed this way and that. They could not go to the garden ever again.

They looked ahead. 'There are lots of weeds here,' said Adam. 'But if we work hard, we can plant crops. We'll manage.'

Eve wiped away a tear. 'It's sad not being friends with God,' she said. 'I hope this mistake is put right one day.'

Noah and the Flood

Long ago, there lived a man named
Noah. He and his wife had three sons.
The three sons each had a wife.
  'Perhaps I'll have grandchildren
soon,' said Noah to himself.
  He began to dream of
happy times ahead.

As Noah sat dreaming, he heard a voice.

'I am unhappy,' said the voice. 'I made a good world, but people nowadays do very bad things.'

'Who's that speaking?' said Noah to himself. 'The one who made the world, hmm?

'Oh! It must be God!'

'I want to begin the world again,' said God to Noah. 'I want you to help me.'

Noah listened carefully to everything God said.

Then Noah went to talk to the family. 'God wants us to build a boat,' he said. 'A very big boat. God has given me instructions and lots of measurements.

'Now to begin, we must fetch some good strong wood...'

The work began. Together they built a boat with three decks and a door. They put waterproof tar on the outside.

'Now we must fetch the animals,' said
Noah. 'A mother and a father
of every kind.'

What a job it was! What a noisy job!

'We need food too,' said Noah.
'Food for us and food for the
animals.'

growl

roar

squeak

tweet tweet

In the end, the work was done.
Everyone and everything were safely
on board.

God shut the door.

The rain started to fall. Pitter-patter,
pitter-patter. Splish-splash.

Soon the rain was tumbling down.
Splosh-splosh-splosh-splosh-splosh-
splosh-splosh.

It rained and rained and rained.
And rained.
The flood began to rise. Up and
up and up. And up.

'Look,' said Noah's wife, 'the whole world is like one big sea.'

'And there's only us left,' said Noah.

He looked down at the grey water.

He looked up at the grey sky.

'I hope God hasn't forgotten us,' said Noah.

God had not forgotten. God sent
a wind that blew and blew.

Whoo-ooh, whoo-ooh, whoo-ooh.

Trickle by trickle, the flood began
to go down until one day…

BUMP.

'We've landed,' announced Noah.
'Somewhere.'

Not long after, they saw they
were on a mountaintop.
Noah sent a raven out
from the boat.
It flapped and flapped
and flew away.

'I'll try again,' said Noah. He sent a
dove out from the boat. The first time
it went, it flew out and flew back. The
second time it went, the dove came
back with an olive leaf.

Everyone on the ark cheered.

'The flood is over,' said God.
'Let the animals go. Tell them
all to have families. I want them
to fill the world again.'
Out they went. What a noise!

'Now it's time for you to go,' said God to Noah. 'You and your family must make new homes for yourselves. You must fill the world with people again.'

Out in the bright, clean world, Noah and his family had a big party.

'Look,' said God. 'I have put a rainbow in the sky. It is the sign of my promise. I will never flood the world again.'

Noah smiled. Now he knew that for ever and ever there would be summer and winter.

For ever and ever there would be a time to sow seeds and a time to harvest crops.

God's world would be a home for
his grandchildren, and his great
grandchildren... for everyone.

Moses and
the Princess

Miriam smiled at her new baby brother.

'He's very special, isn't he?' she said to her mother.

'Very special,' her mother replied.

'We must both take very good care of him.'

There was a problem. Miriam and her family were Israelites. Long ago, the Israelites had been invited to live in Egypt. Now there were lots of them and the Egyptians were afraid of them.

They made them work as slaves.

The king had made a law that all Israelite baby boys must be thrown into the river. His soldiers often came looking.

Miriam's mother made a basket from reeds. She covered it with waterproof tar. She put the baby in the basket and went down to the river.

She hid her baby in his little basket among the reeds.

Miriam hid close by to watch what would happen.

The daughter of the king of Egypt
came down to the river to bathe.
Her servants stood on the bank.

  Suddenly, the princess saw the
basket.

  'Please fetch that for me,' she said.
'I want to know what's inside.'

When the princess lifted the lid,
she saw the baby boy.

'Poor little thing! He's crying!'
she said. 'He's an Israelite baby.
Someone wants to keep him safe.
I'd like to keep him.'

Miriam stepped forward. She spoke up bravely: 'If you like, I can find an Israelite woman to take care of him for you.'

'Yes please,' replied the princess.

Miriam ran home and called to her mother.

'Come quickly,' she said. 'The princess found our baby. She wants to keep him. She needs someone to look after him.'

The two hurried back as fast as they could. The princess gave the mother her own baby.

'Please look after him for me,' she said. 'I will pay you. When the boy is old enough, he will come and live at the palace.'

'His name –' began the mother.

'Oh, yes: what shall I call him?' said the princess. 'I know: Moses.'

Moses grew up to be a prince.
He lived among the Egyptians.
He was rich and powerful.
But he knew he was really an
Israelite.
He was very angry at the way his
people were treated. That got him
into trouble, and he had to run away.

In the faraway desert, Moses
became a shepherd. One day he
saw a strange sight: a bush was
on fire, but none of it was really
burning.

The fire was a sign that God was
there. God spoke to Moses.

'I want you to rescue my people.
Tell the king of Egypt to let them
go free.'

Moses went and asked his brother Aaron to help him. Together they went to see the king of Egypt.

'If you don't let our people go, God will send all sorts of trouble,' they pleaded.

'No,' said the king. 'No, no, no and no.'

There was one disaster after another: frogs hopping everywhere, flies buzzing everywhere, locusts chewing everywhere. The king would not change his mind.

The troubles got worse. The king changed his mind. Moses led his people out of Egypt, away from the cruel king.

Suddenly, the king changed his mind again. 'Hurry!' he told his army. 'Drive your chariots as fast as you can. Go and get them back.'

The people saw the army behind them.

They saw a sea in front of them.
Moses lifted his stick, and God made
a path for them through the sea.

Safe on the other side, Miriam
danced and played the tambourine.
'God has saved us,' she sang, and
everyone joined in.

David and Goliath

David was the youngest in his family. Like everyone, he had to help on the family farm.

His job was to look after the sheep.

While he watched them, he liked to sing. Sometimes he played his harp.

Sometimes he practised throwing
stones with his sling.

He was a good shot.

He needed to be a good shot:
sometimes wild animals came
and tried to steal his sheep.

David slung stones at them to
make them go away.

One day, David's father sent him on an errand.

'Your brothers have been away in the king's army for a long time. Go to see if they are well. They will not have much food left. Here is bread and cheese to take them.'

David set off. He found the soldiers lining up, ready to fight.

David hurried to find his brothers.

Across the valley, an enemy soldier was marching forward. He wore heavy armour. He carried a huge spear.

'I am Goliath!' shouted the enemy soldier. 'Come and fight me! Beat me, and you will win the war. Lose, and you will become our slaves.

'Ha, ha, ha! Ha, ha, ha! Ha, ha, ha!'

The king's soldiers began to run.
'Look at him!' they said to each other.

'Would you fight that giant soldier?
The king will give a big reward to the
man who does.'

'Tell me more!' said David eagerly.
'We shouldn't be scared. We are
God's people.'

One of David's brothers heard him talking. 'Cheeky brat!' he said. 'You should be at home with the sheep.'

David kept asking questions.
Someone took him to see King Saul.

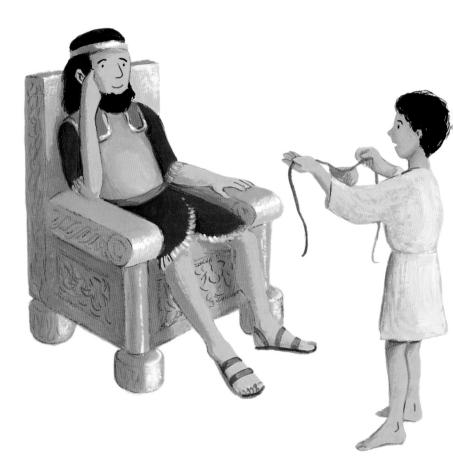

'Your Majesty,' said David. 'No one should be afraid of that soldier. I will go and fight him.'

Saul sighed. 'You're just a boy!' he said.

'I can fight bears and lions,' said David. 'I stop them stealing my sheep.'

In the end, the king let David go. He took his stick and his sling.

He stopped by a stream to pick up five small pebbles.

Goliath came marching down. His shield bearer marched in front of him.

'Come on! Come and fight!' jeered Goliath. 'You'll be a tasty meal for the vultures!'

David stood up. 'You've got a sword, a spear and a javelin,' he called. 'But I trust in God.'

Then he put a stone in his sling.

He whirled the sling above his head.

He threw the stone.

It hit Goliath sharply. The giant fell down.

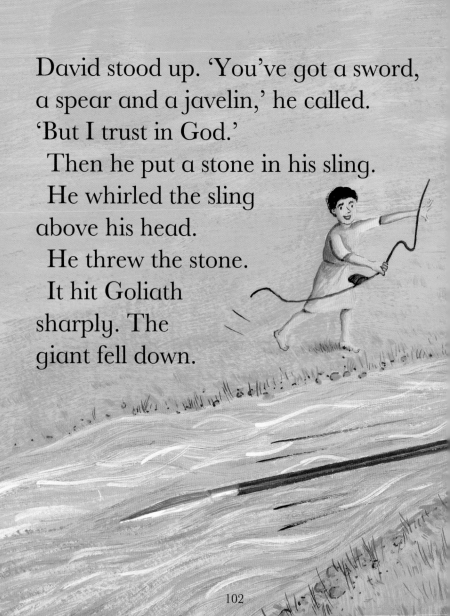

The army behind David cheered.
'We've won! We've won!'

The enemy army in front of David
began to run away. Saul's army
chased them all the way back to
their own cities.

David became a famous soldier.
He won many battles for his people.
When King Saul died, David
became the next king.

He had a beautiful palace. He
was very rich.

He didn't have to worry about
sheep. He didn't have to worry
about wild animals.

He still liked singing. He still liked playing the harp.

He still put his trust in God.

'I shall write a song,' he said to himself. 'It will tell everyone about God and God's goodness.'

Dear God, you are my shepherd,
You give me all I need,
You take me where the grass
  grows green
And I can safely feed.

You take me where the water
Is quiet and cool and clear;
And there I rest and know I'm safe
For you are always near.

Jonah and the Whale

Jonah was a prophet. When God spoke, Jonah listened. Then he told other people God's message.

One particular day, God asked Jonah to do something.

'Go to Nineveh. The people there do wicked things. Tell them I've noticed how bad they are.'

Jonah frowned. 'Hmph,' he said. 'The people of Nineveh are our enemies.'

'In fact,' he said to himself, 'I won't go.'

Jonah knew which road led to Nineveh. He went the other way, to a town called Joppa.

Down by the harbour was a boat. It was ready to sail to Spain.

'I'll go there!' said Jonah.

He paid his fare and climbed on board.

That night, a storm blew up.

'RRAAHH,' roared the wind.

'CRRRASSHH,' went the waves.

'Help! We're sinking,' cried the sailors. 'Help! Help!'

The captain found Jonah asleep.

'Get up and pray!' he ordered. 'Ask your god to save us.'

The sailors were all praying, but the storm grew worse.

'A powerful god is angry with one of us,' said a sailor. 'Let's do the choosing game to find out who.'

It was Jonah.

'I'm sorry,' he said. 'I'm running away from God. You'll have to throw me overboard.'

The sailors tried to row the ship to shore, but it was no good.

They shouted to heaven. 'O God, whoever you are, we're really sorry. Please don't blame us!'

Then they picked Jonah up and threw him into the sea.

Splash!

The little ship sailed safely away.
 Jonah sank deep down among the
seaweed and the fishes.
 Then…

gulp

'Oh,' said Jonah. 'I thought that was the end of me. But suddenly everything has changed.

'I think I've been swallowed by a most enormous fish.

'It must be a miracle. Well… in that case, I'd better say a prayer.'

He began.

'Thank you, God, for saving me. I'm very sorry. Please keep me alive, and then I'll do what you want.'

He waited and waited and waited. Then he felt himself being thrown forwards.

'Help!' he began.

The fish spat Jonah onto a beach.

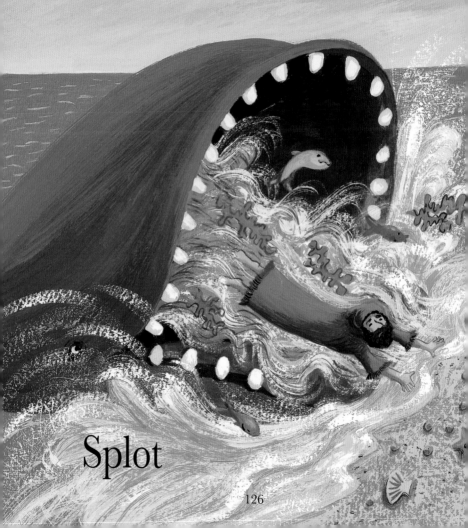

Splot

Jonah went straight to Nineveh.
'Listen up, you Ninevites!' cried
Jonah. 'God says this: you have
been very wicked. In forty days,
God will destroy your city.'
'Oh my!' said the people of Nineveh.
'Oh dear! Oh no! Oh help!'

The King of Nineveh called all the people together.

'Listen everyone,' he announced. 'We must show God we are sorry.

'No one is to eat anything. Everyone is to wear scratchy sackcloth. All of us must pray to God.

'Most of all, we must stop doing wicked things. Then, perhaps, God will forgive us.'

'I'm pleased,' said God. 'I think I'll forgive them.'

Jonah heard what God said and it made him cross.

'I knew it, God,' he said. 'That's what I was afraid you'd do.'

Jonah stomped out of the city.

He found a place to sit. He wanted to watch what happened next.

The sun shone brightly.

'Phew, it's hot here,' he said to himself. 'I need to make a shelter.'

He worked all day. The shelter was good, but Jonah was still hot.

'I wish there was some shade,' he said. 'Oh… look at that plant! It's growing before my very eyes.'

Jonah watched as the plant grew round his shelter. He watched the leaves unfold. They were huge and gave lovely cool shade.

'This is very nice,' said Jonah. 'Perhaps things aren't so bad after all.'

The next day, Jonah heard a sound.

Munch,
munch,
munch!

A worm came and chewed the stem and the leaves. Very soon, the plant died.

'My poor plant!' cried Jonah. 'Now I'll have no shade when the sun gets hot.'

The day grew hotter and hotter.
'It's horrible out here,' said Jonah.
'I wish I were dead.'

Then he heard God speaking.

'Why are you angry about the plant, Jonah?

'I was the one who made it grow for you. You did nothing. Yet you feel sorry for it.'

'I do indeed!' said Jonah.

'I made the people of Nineveh,' said God. 'There are thousands of them. Grown ups, children – and all their animals. I feel sorry for them. That is why I am going to forgive them.'

Daniel and the Lions

Daniel was a very important man. He helped King Darius rule his empire.

He worked hard, and he was very good at his job.

'I think I shall put Daniel in charge of the empire,' said Darius.

The other people who worked for Darius were very cross.

'Why is Daniel getting a better job?' they muttered. 'How we wish he would make a big mistake! Then we could get rid of him.'

'You know,' said one, 'I've got an idea. Listen to my secret plan.'

They huddled close together and whispered.

Then they went to King Darius.

'Your Majesty,' they said. 'May you live for ever.

'You are great. You are wonderful. You are like a god.'

'Thank you very much,' said Darius.

'We want you to make a law,' said the men. 'No one may pray to anyone except to you. If anyone disobeys, they will be thrown into a den of lions.'

'What a splendid idea,' said Darius. 'It will be one of my great laws that cannot be changed.'

Daniel always prayed to God.
  In the morning, he prayed to God.
  In the middle of the day, he prayed
to God.
  At the end of the day, he said this
prayer:

'When I lie down, I sleep in peace.
Dear God, you always keep me safe.'

Daniel was not alone. The people he worked with were watching.

The next day, they went to see King Darius.

'Your Majesty,' they said. 'May you live for ever.

'Do you remember the law you made?'

'I do,' said Darius. 'It's a very strict law: no ifs, no buts, no changes.'

'Indeed it is,' said the men. 'If anyone breaks it, you will throw them into a den of lions.'

'I will,' said Darius. Then, for a bit of fun, he roared. 'Hooraaaaaah!'

'Your Majesty,' said the men.

'Daniel has broken the law. He keeps on saying prayers to his God.'

Darius stopped making roaring noises. He looked very sad. 'I don't want Daniel eaten,' he said. 'He's a very good worker. He's not included in the law.'

'Oh, but Your Majesty,' said the men. 'You CANNOT change the law.'

Darius frowned. 'Let me think,' he said. 'I'm going to find a reason why he shouldn't be included.'

He was thinking as the sun rose high in the sky. One of the men popped in to see him.

'Daniel's saying his midday prayers,' said the man.

'Go away, I'm still thinking,' said Darius.

He was thinking as the sun sank low. The same man popped back.

'Daniel's saying his evening prayers,' he said.

'Bother,' said Darius. 'It's the den for Daniel.'

Soldiers went to fetch Daniel and threw him to the lions.

Darius came to see him. 'It's all a bit of a mistake,' he called to Daniel. 'I hope your God will keep you safe.'

'Excuse me, Your Majesty,' said a soldier. 'Please move along. I'm going to block the opening to the den.

'We don't want anyone to let Daniel out, do we?'

Darius did not sleep that night.
  'Oh dear, oh dear, oh dear,' he muttered. He paced up and down.
  'Do you want a meal?' asked a servant. 'Or some wine?'

'No thank you,' said the king.
'Shall I play some music for you?'
asked another servant.
'Stop trying to cheer me up,' said
Darius. 'It just makes me more cross.'

Down in the pit, Daniel was sitting among the shadows. He couldn't see anything very clearly, but he felt sure someone was there with him. Whoever it was seemed to have a special power over the lions.

First they yawned huge, scary yawns. Then they gave little growls and fell asleep.

As soon as it was light, the king hurried to the pit.

'Daniel?' he called. 'Did your God save you?'

'May Your Majesty live for ever!' replied Daniel. 'God sent an angel to save me from the lions.'

'Hoorah!' cried Darius. This time, he didn't roar.

He helped pull Daniel to safety. 'Fetch the men who tried to kill Daniel,' he said to the soldiers. 'Put them in the pit instead.'

Then King Darius sent a message
to everyone in his empire.

'There is no god like Daniel's God.

'Daniel's God is strong and works
miracles to save people.

'Everyone must respect Daniel's
God.'

Daniel went back to his old job,
and he did it very, very well.

The First Christmas

Long ago, in the little town of Nazareth, there lived a girl named Mary.

She grew up believing in God. She grew up wanting to do the things that are right and good.

As she grew up, she looked forward to getting married. It was all arranged that she would marry Joseph.

One day, an angel came to her with a message.

'God has blessed you,' said the angel. 'You are going to have a baby boy: Jesus. He will do wonderful things. People will say he is the Son of God.'

Mary was puzzled. 'I'm not married yet,' she explained.

'God will make everything come true,' said the angel.

'I will be happy to do what God wants,' replied Mary.

Joseph was upset by Mary's news.

'Mary's baby isn't my baby,' he said. 'Perhaps I shouldn't marry her.'

That night, he had a dream. An angel spoke to him:

'Please look after Mary and her baby. Everything will be all right.'

Soon after, Joseph went to find Mary. 'I still want us to be husband and wife,' he said to her.

'Now, I know you've heard about the emperor – that he wants to have a new list of all the people in his empire.

'I want us to go to my home town of Bethlehem together. There we shall put our names on the list as a family.'

When they got to Bethlehem, there was a problem.

'No one has any spare room,' explained Joseph. 'We have to shelter in an animal shed.'

That night, Mary's baby, Jesus, was born. She wrapped him up snugly.

'This manger can be his cradle,' said Joseph.

On the hills nearby were some shepherds. They were looking after their sheep.

They were watching for danger. Who could tell what lurked in the shadows?

Suddenly, the sky was bright. An angel appeared. 'Don't be afraid,' said the angel. 'I have good news. A baby has been born in Bethlehem. He will bring God's blessings to all the world. Go and find him. He's sleeping in a manger.'

Then more and more angels appeared, all singing to God.

All of a sudden, the angels disappeared. Everything was dark again.

'Let's go to Bethlehem,' said the shepherds.

They went and found Mary and Joseph and the baby.

Everything was just as the angel had said.

Not very far away was the city of Jerusalem. Some people had gone on a long journey to see the king there.

'We're following a star,' they said. 'It is shining because a new king has been born. Is he here?'

The king frowned and shook his head. 'There's an old story that the greatest king ever will be born in Bethlehem,' he said.

'I want you to go there. If you find a new king, be sure to tell me where he is.'

The men set out for Bethlehem.

'I hope this is the right way,' said one.

'Oh look!' said a second. 'There's our star again!'

'I'm glad we've come,' said a third. 'I think we've been very wise.'

The star shone down on a little house in Bethlehem.

The wise men went inside. They saw Mary and her baby.

'This is the king we have been looking for!' they said.

They gave him gifts: gold, frankincense and myrrh.

That night, they dreamed the same dream. An angel told them not to go back to the king. They agreed to go home a different way.

Soon after, Joseph came hurrying to Mary and Jesus.

'I love you both so much,' he said. 'Now a dream has got me worried. I'm afraid we won't be safe here in Bethlehem. Let's leave at once.'

The three of them journeyed on.

Mary held Jesus tight. After all that had happened, she felt sure of one thing:

Her little baby must truly be God's own Son, and she would keep him safe.

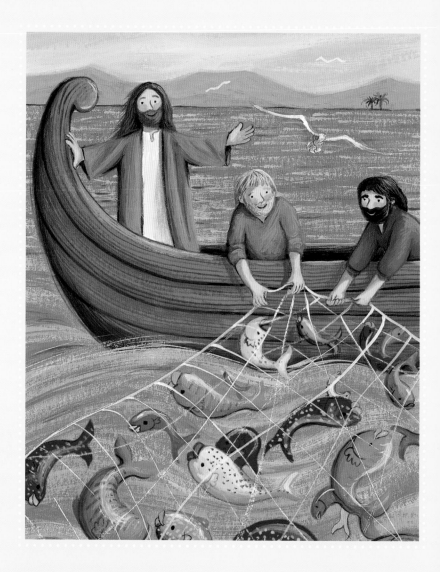

Jesus and
the Fishermen

Jesus grew up in Nazareth.

Like everyone else, he went to the synagogue each week.

He listened as the teacher read from the holy books.

He listened as the teacher talked about God.

When Jesus was a man, he became a teacher too.

People from other towns asked him to come and teach in their synagogues.

He read from the holy books.

He talked about God and God's love.

More and more people wanted to hear what he had to say. Jesus began to spend every day teaching.

One day, Jesus was teaching by Lake Galilee. Lots of people came to listen. The people at the back couldn't see him.

Jesus saw two fishing boats on the beach. 'Please let me use a boat,' said Jesus to the fishermen. 'I'll get on, and you push it into the water. Then everyone will be able to see me.'

At the end of the day, Jesus called to one of the fishermen. 'Simon, come and let the fishing nets into the water. You and your friends will catch a lot of fish.'

'No we won't,' said Simon. 'We didn't catch any last night.'

'Try,' said Jesus.

They caught more fish than the nets could hold.

Suddenly, the fishermen felt rather scared of Jesus. 'I don't think I'm good enough to be your friend,' said Simon.

'I want all of you to be my friends,'
said Jesus. 'You're very good at
gathering fish in nets. I need you to
help me gather people: people who
want to be part of God's family.'

The fishermen came: Simon and his brother Andrew; James and his brother John.

Later, Jesus chose eight more people to help him, making twelve special friends.

Jesus and his friends often went by boat. It was a good way to get to other towns beside Lake Galilee.

Jesus wanted to teach in lots of places.

One evening, Jesus and his friends set off by boat.

The fishermen were in charge of sailing it.

Jesus went to lie down with his head on a pillow. Soon he fell asleep.

In the night, a strong wind began
to blow.

It blew the water into waves.

The wind and the waves tossed the
boat. Jesus' friends were very scared.

'Wake up, Jesus! Wake up!'
they cried. 'You've got to help
us or we'll die.'

Jesus stood up in the boat.
  He spoke to the wind:
'Be quiet!'
  He spoke to the waves:
'Be still!'

At once, the lake was calm.

'Why were you scared?' asked Jesus.
'Do you not have faith in God?'

The eight friends looked at the four fishermen. 'Did you think it was a scary storm?' they asked.

'Yes,' said the fishermen. 'But not as scary as what Jesus just did.'

They all began to wonder the same thing: Who can Jesus be? How can he do miracles like that?

Jesus and the Prayer

One day, Jesus saw that crowds had come to see him.

He went to the top of a hill near Lake Galilee. Everyone sat down to listen.

'Are you here because you want to be God's friend?' he asked. 'If you are, you can feel truly happy.

'God welcomes you into the kingdom of heaven!

'God's friends should always want to do good – even to people they don't like.

'Even to people who are cruel to them.

'The Roman soldiers are allowed to ask us to carry their heavy packs for one whole mile.

'When that happens, offer to carry it for two miles.

'Take time alone to pray to God. Say this:

'Our Father in heaven,
hallowed be your name,
your kingdom come,
your will be done,
on earth as in heaven.
Give us today our daily bread.
Forgive us our sins
as we forgive those who sin against us.
Lead us not into temptation
but deliver us from evil.'

'You must always forgive people, even if they have been very bad to you. Then you can be sure that God will forgive you.

'Don't waste your time trying to be rich. God will make sure you have all you need.

'Look at the birds. They don't sow seeds or gather a harvest.

'Even so, God takes care of them.

'Look at the flowers. They don't spend their time weaving and sewing.

'Even so, the petals they wear are lovelier than the finest clothes.

'God cares about petals that last a day. God cares even more about you.

'I can see you all listening, and that is good.

'You must also do what I say.

'I will tell you a story. It is about two men who each wanted to build a house.

' "I want my house now," said one. "This sandy soil down by the river is easy to dig.

' "I won't have to carry my building things far."

'His house was ready in no time. He had a lovely, lazy summer.

' "I want my house to last," said the other.

' "I will build my house up here on the rock."

'It was hard work. He had to chip out the foundations with a hammer.

'He had to carry his building things up high.

'By the time he had finished, the summer had gone.

'Then came winter: the wind blew cold, the rain hissed down.

'The river rose higher and higher.
'It overflowed its banks.
'Soon it was lapping around the house on the sandy soil.

'Suddenly a wave came tumbling down the river. It swept the house away.

'"Oh, how foolish I was," cried the man.

'Up on the rock, the other man nodded sadly.

' "I think I made the wise choice," he said. "My house is safe. It is truly going to last. The storms will not reach it." '

Jesus looked at the crowds. 'If you listen to what I say and then forget it, you are like the foolish man.

'If you listen to what I say and obey it, you are like the wise man.

'You will do wonderful things with your life, and God will bless you.'

Jesus and the Miracle

One day, Jesus went to the town of Capernaum. The news spread quickly.

'Look – Jesus is here! He's staying at the same house as before. All kinds of people are going to hear him speak.'

'Hurry! There won't be much room left.'

A mother and her daughter watched as the crowds hurried by.

'Why are those men carrying that man down the street on his mattress?' asked the little girl.

'The poor man cannot walk,' replied her mother. 'But I wonder where they are taking him?'

'Oh! I think I can guess!'

'They want to see Jesus. Look at the crowds who have come to see him!'

'Everyone says that Jesus can work miracles,' said the little girl's mother. 'I think the men want Jesus to heal their friend.'

'But how can they get to Jesus?' asked the little girl. 'The house is crowded. No one wants to let them in.'

The four men were puzzled too.

'We can't get in the door,' said one.

'We can't get NEAR the door,' said the second.

'And those steps only go to the roof,' said the third.

'LET'S GO TO THE ROOF!' said the fourth.

The roof was flat. The men started digging into it.

'What's the plan?' asked the man on the mattress.

'The plan is to take you to Jesus,' said the friends.

Soon they had dug deep into the roof.

One of the men fetched some rope.
They tied a length to each corner
of the mattress.

'Now we must do the last bit
quickly,' said another of the men.
'Ready – GO!'

They made the hole go right
through the ceiling.

They lowered their friend down
on his mattress.

'I can see people smiling…' said
one of the men on the roof.

'I don't see everybody smiling,'
said another.

Jesus spoke to the man on the bed. 'Your sins are forgiven,' he said.

The people next to Jesus began to whisper.

'Did you hear? Jesus said the man was forgiven for all the bad things he has ever done.'

'Tut, tut. Only God can forgive like that.'

'Jesus isn't a proper teacher. We're proper teachers. We know what's right.'

257

Jesus looked at the teachers.

'I know what you're thinking,' he said.

'You don't like me saying, "Your sins are forgiven." But I'm going to show you something. What I say really is what God wants to say.'

He turned to the man on the bed. 'Get up, pick up your bed, and go home!'

The man on the bed could see Jesus' kind face.

He could see the teachers frowning.

He could see his friends waving down to him.

He knew he must try to sit up.

He did sit up.

He stood up.

He took a step. Then he danced a little jig around the mattress!

He bent down and rolled the mattress into a bundle.

'See you outside,' called his friends.

'Thank you, God! Thank you, Jesus! Thank you, friends!' the man was singing.

'Hooray! Hooray!' cried his friends.

'Look,' said the little girl to her mother. 'The man is carrying his mattress now. He can walk very well.'

'So Jesus really can heal people,'
said her mother. 'No wonder they
believe he is God's son.'

The Lost Sheep

One day, a crowd of people came
to listen to Jesus.

There were all kinds of people.
Some were rich. Some were poor.
Some always obeyed the law.
Some were always in trouble.

Some of the people were rather
proud of themselves.

'Do you know what annoys me
about coming to see Jesus?'
whispered one of them. 'We always
end up sitting close to the wrong
kind of person.'

'I know,' answered another. 'Jesus seems to like them. It makes me wonder – perhaps he's the wrong kind of person too.'

Jesus knew what they were thinking. He started telling a story.

'There was once a man who had 100 sheep.

'He counted his sheep every evening, as he let them run into the sheepfold.

'"Stay inside," he used to say to them. "I don't want any wild animals to steal you away.

"If any come near, I'll be here to scare them off."

'He counted his sheep every morning, when he led them out of the sheepfold.
'"Come on," he used to say. "We must go down to the stream where you can drink."

'He counted his sheep in the daytime,
as they nibbled the green grass.
' "Bother," he said one day. "I think
I got the numbers muddled.

"I only counted to 99. I'm going to count again."

'He counted very carefully. To his dismay, there were only 99 sheep left.

' "Oh dear," he said. He picked up his shepherd's stick.

' "I'm going to have to go and find my lost sheep."

'He left the green fields and went up into the hills. He looked among the rocks. He looked among the thorn bushes.

'He looked everywhere.

'At last he found his lost sheep. He was overjoyed.

'He picked it up and carried it back to the flock.

'As he came home that day, he called out to his friends.

 '"Look! This is the sheep I lost. I found it.

 '"Come round to my house tonight. I'm going to have a party."'

Jesus looked at the proud people. He looked at the people who always seemed to be in trouble.

'God is like that shepherd,' said Jesus. 'God cares about the people who get things wrong. God goes looking for them, so they can be part of God's family again.'

When that happens, the angels in heaven are as happy as can be.

The First Easter

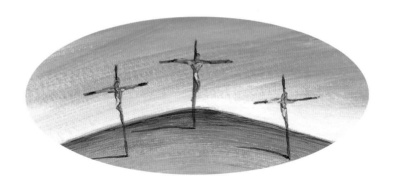

It was nearly time for the biggest festival of the year.

'Let's go to Jerusalem,' said Jesus to his friends. 'That's the best place to be at festival time.'

Jesus rode to the city on a donkey. People began to whisper. 'Look! Jesus is riding to Jerusalem. He looks like a king!'

'God bless the king!' shouted
someone. Everyone began to cheer.
They cut palm branches and waved
them like flags.

Jesus went through the city gate that led to the Temple.

It was like being in a marketplace. There were even live animals for sale.

'This is all wrong,' said Jesus to the stallholders. 'Get out at once!

'The Temple is meant to be a place of prayer. You just want to make money.'

He chased everyone out.

The people in charge of the Temple frowned. 'Jesus is a troublemaker,' they grumbled.

'How can we get rid of him?'

Not long after, a man named Judas came to see them. He was meant to be one of Jesus' best friends. 'I can tell you when it's a good time to catch him,' he whispered.

The time came for the festival meal.
There was bread and wine on the
table. Jesus took each in turn and
shared it with his twelve friends.

'Tonight, God is making a promise,'
he said.

'It's a promise for everyone who
follows me and obeys me. One day,
you will eat and drink at my table
in my kingdom.'

His friends didn't really understand.
They just talked noisily. Except for
Judas, who slipped away.

After the meal, Jesus and the rest of his friends went to a quiet hillside. It was night. The olive trees cast dark shadows.

Alone and quietly, Jesus prayed to God.

'I know that terrible things are about to happen,' he prayed. 'I wish there were another way to make everything work out… but there isn't.'

Suddenly, Judas arrived.

With him were some of the people in charge of the Temple and some of the Temple guards.

They took Jesus away. They paid people to tell lies about him and say he had done wrong things.

They marched him off to the ruler of Jerusalem, who was called Pontius Pilate.

'This Jesus is a rebel – he does wrong things,' they said. 'He must die.'

Pilate didn't really believe them. 'Is that what you and the people really want?' he asked.

'Yes it is,' everyone shouted. 'Crucify him!'

Pilate gave the order for Jesus to die.

Soldiers took Jesus away and nailed him to a cross.

From the cross Jesus said a prayer.
'Forgive them, Father! They don't know what they are doing.'

He looked at the people standing nearby. There was his mother, Mary, and next to her, his loyal friend John.

'Please take care of my mother when I'm gone,' said Jesus. John nodded, and put his arm round Mary.

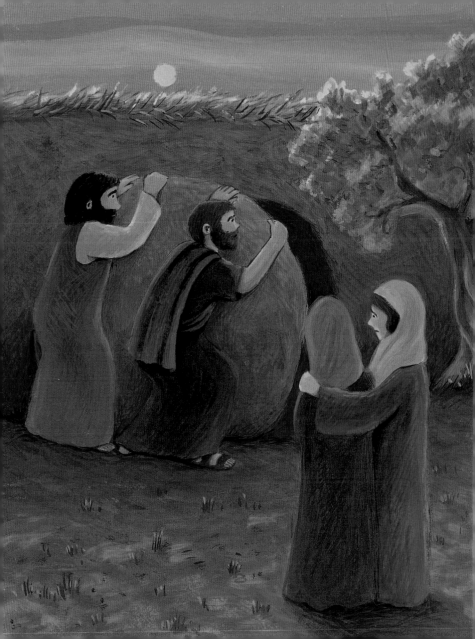

The hours went by. Jesus died on the cross. A man named Joseph came and took the body.

He and his helpers laid it in a tomb that was like a cave.

The tomb had a round stone door. They rolled it shut. They had to hurry, because the weekly day of rest began at sunset.

The day after the day of rest was Sunday.

Some of the women who had followed Jesus came back to the tomb.

'What has happened?' they cried. 'Why is the door open?'

'Why is the tomb empty?'

Suddenly, two people in bright shining clothes appeared.

'Jesus isn't here,' they said. 'He's alive again.'

Not long after, they all saw him alive again.

'My work is done,' said Jesus. 'You have listened to everything I told you about God. You have seen miracles. You have seen me alive again.

'Now you must go and tell the world about all you have learned.

'God will make you wise and brave.'

Then he said a blessing prayer and was taken up into heaven.

Jesus' followers didn't feel wise or brave. They wanted to hide indoors. Then came the festival called Pentecost. Early in the morning, when they were indoors together, they heard a noise like a strong wind blowing.

They saw something like flames of fire dancing overhead.

Suddenly, they knew for sure that God was with them.

They hurried out to tell all the world about Jesus and his message.

The news is still spreading.